Sally's Casserole

Collection of Poems by
Sally Love Saunders

ISBN: 978-1-09839-340-3

SALLY LOVE SAUNDERS is a widely published poet, lecturer, workshop leader and author of six poetry books. Born in 1940, she wrote her first poem at the age of six, and has pursued that passion throughout her life. Studying in Japan after college, and during travel which introduced her to Nehru in India and Albert Schweitzer in Africa, as well as teaching stints among migrant farm laborers, children in Appalachia, and time teaching on the Navajo Reservation, her conviction that poetry offers a universal way to express what is in your soul has remained unchallenged.

As one of the 'founding fathers' of The National Association for Poetry Therapy, Sally has spoken at many conferences familiarizing health care professionals with her unique approach to teaching poetry writing. She lectured on the Healing Power of Poetry at the University of California Medical Center, San Francisco, CA. Also, she gave a talk to doctors on Poetry Therapy at a poetry conference at the St. Francis Hotel in San Francisco.

In the course of her career, she has received numerous city, state and private grants for Poetry Therapy in libraries, schools and state institutions, including the Institute at the Pennsylvania Hospital. She worked there for many years, helping people heal through the creation of poetry, expressing their inner emotions. She taught in a migrant labor camp, helping them to read & write English, as well as creating poetry. The State Department gave her a Title 3 grant to teach Appalachian teachers how to teach poetry writing and the Christian Science Monitor published her lesson plan for teaching poetry.

Sally has developed fun techniques to help individuals to get in touch with their own unique creativity. She was always interested in working with children and was a "Johnny Appleseed Poet"; getting them to think of poetry while playing games and moving around the country to inspire their creativity. As the Poetry Lady, she went from school to school in Philadelphia, working to make poetry fun, and laying the groundwork for a lifetime of interest in poetry. They would play "Poetry Musical Chairs", where the student who sat in the Answer Chair created a line of poetry when the music stopped. She specially requested rooms away from other classes so that students could make noise, stamp their feet, and have fun while creating poetry.

She continues to give poetry readings and run poetry workshops at the Institute for Cultural Integration in the San Francisco Bay area, proving over and over that "we are all poets who only need to learn how to access that inner spark". She gives monthly poetry readings via conference calls and continues to write her own poems. She has written over 8,000 poems.

Sally's poetry and articles have appeared in over three hundred fifty recognized publications, both literary and scholarly journals as well as periodicals such as the New York Times International, the London Times, the Denver Post, and the Christian Science Monitor. Sally has six poetry books published and has received many prizes for her poetry. She is also listed in several Who's Who publications including Who's Who of American Women.

CONTENTS

HUMANS BEING HUMAN BEINGS 67

DOCTOR'S ORDERS 93

TIME FOR SPACE & NATURE 115

AGING GRATEFULLY 155

TESTIMONIALS 177

GRATITUDE 181

POETRY
POTPOURRI

A POEM

4/9/1961

A poem is an unexpected house guest,
Who arrives with a suitcase.
Immediately he unpacks,
And settles down.
A poem is an unexpected house guest,
Who recalls old experiences
Suddenly giving them new light.
Yes, a poem is house guest,
For after he is gone
It seems as though he is still there.

A POET

12/26/1961

I am a child
Who runs in
To babble out the messages of insight and glee.
My listeners are words and paper -
Will they pass it onto you
As second-hand news?

"Poor child, who stammers
With flashing eyes and a loud voice,
Only to get tangled up in words and breath.
Child, it may be many years
When you've moved on
That you'll be able to tell your stories clearly."

Poetry - my best friend.
I can pull you up
around my ears
and shield out the world.

You cozy my life
giving me a fireplace
when I need it.
Poetry my center.

ON CREATIVITY

9/26/1993

Creativity - So many ideas
Flying around like colorful butterflies
on the green garden of my mind.
Erect my butterfly net; my pen
Chasing first one idea then another
So many ideas fly un-captured.

I feel a poem coming on;
A need to sneeze - cry.
Write!   Yes!   Write...
Remembering the barn at Idlewild Farm;
how the barn swallows
left a lot -
leaving their dirty droppings.
I've felt like a barn lately
with friends, family and acquaintances
flying away.
Flying high and off with a lot of power.
I'm an empty cold barn.
in need of roosting barn swallows.
Perhaps my tears will
heal the cracking paint.
The sun holds me in its arms;
its rays stroking and comforting.
But for now
I'm a cold lonely barn.

EVENING CONCERT

11/17/1994

There is music from their writing
beautiful soothing music.
The silence so moving.
I'm held in mother's arms
of beautiful thoughts.
I, the leader won't disturb
the evening insects singing.
Allowing them to not be disturbed
gives them power.
They don't need to be rushed,
just allowed to sing with their pens.

A PROUD PARENT

6/8/1996

Poems -
Are my babies.
grow from me.
I tend to them.
Don't know
if they will grow up straight
or strong
or not.
First time see them on paper.
Like nurse bringing to new mother
in delivery room.
In a book
their graduation day.

2/4/2006

I'm happiest right here
with my poetry gatherings
Enjoying the gems of their hearts
and souls.
I'm happiest
like a bird in a bird bath
here at Cultural Integration Fellowship
with my poetry gatherings.

3/6/2012

A poem is caught in my throat
the ink on pen dry
for some reason words won't flow
frozen feelings
like a very icy day in New Hampshire.
Long for thaw of words
with gushing movement
Until free of what's trapped inside.

Poems like gold nuggets
from gold panning.
The dirt disappears
away
and nuggets remain
So tiny but golden.

Bringing newborn poems
to Sacred Ground--
a baptism
a baby/poem shower.
You Sacred Grounders
godparents and family
to my new poem baby.

I feel a poem coming on
Like the ocean curling into itself
preparing to lunge
and splash
Covering all rocks nearby
I feel a poem coming on
My back arched up like a cat
ready to hiss and spray
I feel a poem coming on
soon there will be angry cloudburst
of rain words drenching words
plenty of rain words.
I feel a poem coming on
soon--very soon.

Poem ready to be born
Comes at its own time
like a baby ready to be born
I must not stop.
poetry struggling to be born
when water breaks
pen and paper needed
Do not abort a poem!
All screaming and kicking poems
must be given life.

Poetic thoughts gurgling
but stuttering
pen cannot catch
these poetic thoughts flit around
like electric tiddleywinks
so I bring cooling balm of paper
to catch them like a safety net
and they land nicely on paper.
Phew!

We gathered at his feet
as siblings do to parent
or grand parent
who reads and tells stories.
Greg, our father
nourishes us
and we are delighted
amused
warmly touched
our separate responses harmonize.

NO PLEASURE SWEETER

11/9/2019

No pleasure sweeter
than reading my poetry
to others.
I feel like a mother
showing off her child.
perhaps her child wearing dress clothes
perhaps playing in a piano concert.
A proud parent am I.

A poem knocks at the door or my mind
not now, I lazily reply
am half asleep
Later
there is no later
I want to come in now
and be seen.
Later I will have vanished.

I AM A WORD PAINTER

I am a word painter.
I carve sentences
out of soapstone
and run my hand over them
until they are smooth.

I am a balloon woman.
Many colorful balloons
follow me -
I can choose which idea
which plan
or which person to see
at whim.
Easily I can let one balloon float away,
and I can let the air out.
I would like to be a squirrel
easily running up and down tree trunks.

I am a gold panner.
Finding gold nuggets of poetry
in people who thought
there weren't any.

I am a poet -
words are my craft.
Like a blacksmith,
I hammer and hammer away

I AM A WORD PAINTER CONT'D.

until the lines fit.
Into the furnace of my mind
they go,
and out into the cool
onto the metal working space.

Sometimes I'm a glass blower,
the fire of my feelings
forging shapes and forms.

Sometimes I'm a smiling,
toothless, six year-old
with pigtails, saucer eyes and a big smile.

Sometimes I'm an adolescent
moody
wondering.
Who am I?
Who am I?
I am the question
not the answer.

You asked me if I was writing
poetry these days.
My hands are holding Kleenex
and more Kleenex.
They are not holding
pen and paper.
I hope soon I can put
the Kleenex away
and write again.
I hope I can turn
my pain into words
and images.

SOLITUDE & THE
SOUNDS OF SILENCE

5/27/1989

A chance to be cupped
in nature's palm
Cradled into sleep
while branches hum
me a lullaby.
Time to just breathe
and let my edges melt.
My alarm clock is far away
Just here covered
with the blue satin quilt of the sky.

1/27/2010

I really love
very early mornings
when the world is asleep
and sleeping quietly.
I have the world to myself
no appointments
no schedule
Time to frolic in being
As if on a beach.

2 a.m. soul delicious time
I swim in the sea of solitude
Cool air no intrusions
can enjoy totally the silence.
The world belongs to me
I'm queen of the mountain.
No one in my wide desert
Lungs can breathe in smoothness.
Rejuvenating and replenishing.

ME TODAY
7/20/2012

I'm empty like a gourded
pumpkin
empty and hollow
and silent.
Stress has carved out
and tossed my blood and veins.
All that is left is empty
empty shell
not even a scrap of paper
blowing in the wind.
Forgot to write
my cheeks sink in
and I stare like a Picasso person.

Silence is Miracle Grow
For my green sprouting poems
Green fields of silence
so welcoming
to new crop of poetry.
Abundant sweet silence
is Miracle Grow
for my green sprouting poems.

11/12/2013

Am in a meadow of time and quiet.
Here poem idea can be planted
and grow.
Ideas do not get snuffed out
by scurry of speed
or activity.
In this meadow they can stretch
and walk maybe wobbly at first.

4 a.m.
It is precious time
between neighbors partying
and neighbors getting ready
to go to work.
Even buses are asleep
and the air seems to breathe
when a sleeping cat breathes
4 a.m. is my precious time
when I can spread the wings
of my soul and enjoy
being alive
and can choose what to do.

JUST MYSELF ALONE

2/24/2018

A poem is interrupting my thoughts
A poem is knocking on the door
of my mind.
A poem wants to give voice
NOW
It wants to speak about
how I miss myself
My own company
Silence is golden
but it has been too long
to follow my own current
to float with arms outstretched
to let momentum of my stream carry me.
I miss my own company.
Should I mark on my calendar
on certain days to do nothing?
and X-out those days for intruders?
Missing time to just float
on my own steam,
My own rhythm?
My own spontaneity?
My own unchartered movement?
I'm over peopleized
I need a date with myself
Just myself alone.

A SLOW-MOTION DAY

4/20/2020

A slow-motion day
no cars honking behind me-
Waiting was peaceful,
the sound of summer insects
humming their tunes.
Conclusions weren't forced
today-
Deadlines put aside.
A day to let dreams loose.

EARLY MORNING IS JUICIEST TIME

5/24/2020

Early morning is juiciest time
for me to write
and nibble on my thoughts and imaginings.
I fence this time off
from to-do intruders
of the to-do's honking
at me to move.
Early morning is juiciest time
for me to write
and nibble on my thoughts and imaginings.

IT'S 3 A.M.

6/17/2020

All is quiet
Very quiet
I lie in my bed
cool clear waters of relaxation
flood me in a soft way.
Blessings turn to sweet sugar.
Thoughts as the parade
of kind people unfolding
across the screen of my mind.
Even sirens are asleep.
Soon construction will start
eating up the city,
but for now, all is calm
all is still including my thoughts
and heart.

WAVES WEAVING INTO OTHER WAVES

9/7/2020

Waves weaving into other waves
like our spirits connect
and weave
bob along,
no clocks dictating
just our spirits
floating along silently.
You are able to walk in pace with me.
Just you and me bobbling along
in sweet harmony
in the shade.

FOG CREATES SILENCE

10/9/2020

Fog creates silence
and silence brings me
to zero-balancing spot
of stillness.
Fog lullabies me to sleep.
I listen to the silence
and am renewed.

IT'S 5 A.M.
11/20/2020

It is 5 a.m.
or maybe 6 a.m.
The still quiet air
spiritually cradles me
in its arms.
Words of strength
a friend lent me--
like lending a good book
came to the surface to nourish me.
I am silently humming
and feeling in perfect balance.

AGAIN

12/12/2020

Again what seemed to be
a pesky poem
Buzzed around my ear
this morning
when I was trying
to sleep in.
This pesky fly poem
Had to be given voice
Had to be noticed
and given attention.
So I got up at 6 a.m.
to write this tattle tale poem!

MELANCHOLY

Melancholy,
walking
down the corridor
of my mind,
scuffs and kicks
odd stones.

IN THE PARK

Mist moisturizing the green
while dew drops of freshness
settle on my being.
A squirrel, saying grace
over his food,
doesn't mind the almost rain.
The group I was to join
stayed back due to gray.
I'm here alone -
remembering Wordsworth's solitary walks
in the Lake Country's heavy dew.
A white swan ever white.
All the grass
a green tonic for me.
Thoughts of you
fit in so beautifully here
permeating my mind
as the mist does the green.

A ROSE PETAL

I'd like to slide down a rose petal
On my back
And crouch on the bottom
And then look up.
I'd like to wrap the petal
All around me
Until I am asleep.

SOMETIMES I AM

Sometimes I am a blues writer
Sometimes a blues singer
Sometimes a blue exister
Who can't do anything but watch.

It is these times
That life is like
A sad and empty stage-
The lighting is good.
The background music
Is slow and lonely.
For life and I are one-
Sad, empty and gray.

Life is simple now-
As only an artist can form.
It's a single melody
Played on a single instrument.

Thanks to my sorrows
For it is then
That I am a blues writer
A blues singer
And sometimes a blues exister
Who can't do anything but watch.

My words bring company

SOMETIMES I AM CONT'D.

As I strum them to myself.
It is like having your child
To play with and watch with
As life goes by in front.

Sorrows make you lazy
In a disenchanted way.
Sorrows make you contented
In little things
That never before mattered.

The single melody goes on-

There is no wonder.

I'm floating on the lake
of solitude
cool
smooth waters.
The water mattresses me
ripples coming towards me.
Time doesn't tick here.
The air hums.

I want to talk with you in silences
maybe a sigh
for hour after hour
mile after mile
unfolding
trees passing
monotonous tones of car
rolling along the highway.
I have spun my toes
round and round
now I want to be still.
The black night like cotton
cushioning us a jewel in a box.
Words protect us from saying
what I really want to say.

COPING
WITH COVID

REMEMBERING HOW THE CHICKENS
4/26/2020

Remembering how the chickens
just pecked away
on barnyard ground
looking for morsels of food.
Mostly passed over grains
and stones
and nondescript stuff.
So now I am like a hen
pecking away
in my shelter in place apartment
looking for grains of tasks can do
While mostly passing over ground
Just pecking away
not going anywhere.
At the most just chuckling
nonsensical sounds.
Instead, wish I was a hawk
with wide wings
and a destination
to let me zoom into.

FEELING LIKE A FISH

5/2/2020

Feeling like a fish
in a fish bowl
upon waking.
No punctuation
of what day it is.
Time doesn't matter-
it blurs into the long expanse of days
and months.
I'm swimming around in the fishbowl
of my apartment-
no map, no calendar.
Just swimming around
upon waking
feeling like a fish
in a fish bowl.

MAKING A PEANUT BETTER
AND JELLY SANDWICH
5/23/2020

Made a peanut butter and jelly sandwich
but forgot the jelly
wore out my phone
so all the people can hear
is a garbled-y voice.
So eager for communication
dropped phone in sink water
Now I'm holding onto a sick phone
for carrying my conversations.
What happens if phone dies
like the world is dying around me
and in me?

I NEED COUPLES COUNSELING
6/11/2020

I need couples counseling
for getting along
with myself.
Doing shelter in place for a long time.
I pick on myself
all the things I should be doing.
It is hard to hear
all the time
Nag, nag, nag.
Those cozy calm days
gotten more scarce.
I feel like a married couple-
too much togetherness
with me, myself and I.

THE CLOCK WITH LONG LIZARD TOES

6/14/2020

The clock with long lizard toes
Crawl so steadily
across the face
of the clock.
Little covering
the face of the clock
so big.
No schedule,
no place to go to,
just me and my apartment
feeling safe
but missing the world.

TODAY

I need a vacation
from Covid-19
Close down
And put aside worry.
A day to breathe normally
and not notice my breathing.
A day to be free of Covid-19.
Please-a vacation.
Wish my vacation
from Covid-19
was always.

A MONK JUST SHARED

6/28/2020

A monk just shared with me
he was refreshed because
he attended a silent retreat
for three months.
Yikes!
I've been in shelter-in-place
for three months-
and talking and sighing
and singing.
Would I have been
Better off in silence
than venting and moaning?

HOW DID THE SURVIVORS

6/29/2020

How did the survivors
of sinking Titanic feel
as they were huddled
in the lifeboats?
I wonder
as I feel we are huddled
into lifeboats
of shelter-in-place.
As the world
is sinking from Covid.

3 A.M.

7/28/2020

Avalanche of Covid-19 mud
Covering the world
and my life.
I lie very still
at 3:00 a.m.
All is quiet
Gradually, the frozen mud
of Covid-19
slips away
and a tiny gold gem
appears.
The gold gem
Sings message:
"You are healthy
You are alive
You are vibrant
You have energy
and zest for living.
You are not the Sally
fraught with virus
as you had been in the past
many years ago.

3 A.M. CONT'D.

You are strong
and oh, so healthy.
And besides,
getting healthier
all the time
while others get sick
with the King of Viruses.
The viruses you had caught
in the past
were nameless
and you had them
alone.
Now you soar above
the sick graphs
and crowded hospitals.
Sing of the joy of health."

OVERDOSING ON SHELTER-IN-PLACE

9/14/2020

Even crayons have lost
their bright colors
and now are washed-out hues.
My creativity level is high
on red
along with air quality level.
Both air quality and I
are on red.

I AM A COVID NAG!

10/23/2020

My dear, I am a Covid nag.
You are very kind to say
I am not a nag.
But I am a nag
wanting to protect you
to keep you safe
to preserve your health.
Nagging you is my way
of soldiering and guarding you.
You are very kind
to say I am not a nag
But! I am a Covid nag!

I DO NOT EVEN HAVE A
TINY CASE OF COVID

11/27/2020

Feeling fine and dandy thank the Lord.
Thank the Lord
Not even a tiny case of Covid.
I know there is
such a thing as
a slight cold
versus pneumonia
But I do not even have
a tiny case of Covid.

DECEMBER

12/4/2020

My shock absorbers
aren't as new and flexible
as I wish.
All the changes
in my living altitude
is making me dizzy
and lightheaded.
My shock absorbers
aren't as new and flexible
as I wish.
All these changes
in my living altitude
is making me dizzy and lightheaded.

TOO OFTEN I COUNT

12/10/2020

Too often I count
how many of a
cat's allotted nine lives
do I have left.
Certainly, surviving Covid
counts as almost lost
even though more people
are surviving
than dying of Covid.
But as an octogenarian
I am known to
count on my fingers
how many of my nine lives
I've spent
And how many left.
Well, I'm not spending
one of my lives
on Covid
and Covid is keeping me
from, say, plane crashes
or fatal car accidents.
So, in a way,
Covid is saving me
a life from my
allotted nine lives.

FINALLY

12/10/2020

Finally, am learning a little
how to ride the
bucking bronco horse
of Covid.
I've been at Covid rodeos
for going on nine months.
Trying to ride wild Covid horses
Keep getting thrown off
hard to the ground.
I dust myself off
then try again.
Another Covid news feed
and off the Covid horse again.
Wham! only to ache
but not broken
not killed.
Wish I could tell you
I'm a smooth
Covid rodeo rider
but I'm not.
But!
I'm still alive
still walking
and still whistling.

HUMANS BEING
HUMAN BEINGS

A LOVE SENRYU

My mouth is dry
My lips are chapped;
I am in love.

MY LOVER'S COAT HANGS
IN THE CLOSET
1/4/1991

My lover's coat hangs in the closet.
I don't know
for how long it will hang there,
but it is there now.
His glasses and current crossword puzzle
poised where he left them
when he got tired and went to bed.
My love so able to unpack the tent
of his being
and truly be in a place
then pull up stakes and leave.
I also see other relics from my past
that have survived the currents of time.
I never knew then they would
still be with me
and what I had thought
would be forever has vanished.
So right now, my lover's coat hangs in my closet.
He is asleep.
His glasses are here.
It is very wonderful and beautiful
and gives me great peace
to have him here.

MY LOVER'S COAT HANGS IN
THE CLOSET   CONT'D.

Somehow, I have to accept
his coat may not always hang in my closet,
Somehow, I need to enjoy
and then be able to let go
as wrenchingly painful
to let the tide of change
come and wash away our
beautiful sand castle.

I know I can't replace
a mother or stepmother
or a grandmother
But I am in place loving you
and caring
and proud of you
For the exquisite man
you are
and always have been.

Every single morning
when I wake up
I thank God
for another day.
For the precious gift
of breath
and ability to stand on my feet
and to swallow
and drink coffee.

ENOUGH

6/11/2010

"Enough." A new mantra
I have enough money
I have enough will power
I'll have enough health
I'll have enough money --
that is a sore one I
need to repeat like --
rosary bead that
keeps repeating.

A set designer am I
carefully placing furniture
and mementos
to ignite your memory
and soul
into symphony of
I remember
and yes I know.

MY MOTHER SNORED!

9/8/2012

My mother snored and
it was awful sharing a room
with her
And! When I ran a workshop
At Pendle Hill Conference Center
while everyone was writing,
she snored
like a loud rusty locomotive!
When I saw her dead
she was so quiet not snoring.

II.

If she has gone to a sleep clinic
am sure she would have broken
sleep measuring apparatuses.
One second of her snoring
and alarms would go off
fire engines would come.

BECKY

9/21/2012

Becky, if the fingers of fate
should snuff me out,
Please know I'll never leave you.
I'll be there in a crying toddler
and when her mother picks her up
and comforts her that is us.
I'll be there
as you pass ice cream cone stands.
My gratitude a warm blanket
ready to hug you with warmth anytime.
Becky, if the fingers of fate
should snuff me out,
Please know I'll never leave you.

DAVID

8/31/2017

David knows me inside and out
warts and all and yet
he comes back
and smiles.
A teacher in my life.
He retrains my thinking
and reaction patterns.
David brings endless patience
and kindness.
He is kindness in itself.
I bring him my dirty emotional laundry.
He washes and irons
so easy and returns
with a smile.

MY SISTER'S DEPARTURE

9/5/2017

Her door is shut.
I hear her footsteps
walking away
getting fainter
and faster.
I know her footsteps
will never come back to me.
She is walking down
a very long corridor
to eternity.
I cannot follow her,
But, she came up the corridor
Eleven years before me.

WISH I HAD A LONG FLASHLIGHT

9/14/2020

Wish I had a long flashlight
with a very bright battery
so I can see
your brain cavity
and explore your
vast thought spaces.
Would like to see your machinery.

NON INVOLVEMENT

She goes to the zoo
looks at the animals
but does not feed them.
She goes to the art museum
sees the statues
but doesn't feel them.
She went to the beach
but never allowed
the salt to sting her.
She shook his hand
but never held it.

A FINGER CROSSED EXISTENCE

I am living a fingered-crossed existence.
Is my guardian angel on vacation?

AN ALCOHOLIC

He drinks so much
Because his insides are on fire.

OLDE RED

I remember Red, the old farm horse,
and his irritation in summer,
when those big black horse flies
would fly to him.
His whole skin shriveling up tight
and his sharp tail
angrily would swat at them hard.
The flies would try again
only again to cause his skin to reject.
And so with you -
When I express my feelings,
I can feel your being cringing up
and feeling most uncomfortable.
Just like Olde Red with the flies
in the heat of summer.

MATCHES

(Brownstone Inn)

We sat at a table
in a restaurant
for hours.
Apart -
while these matches
lay together
very close.
Sometimes they enflame.
Sometimes ashes.
They have a cover
and are stapled together.
Our only togetherness
is in my imagination.
Yet my imaginings - solo
are lonely.

My only intimacy these days
is in the theater of my mind.
I don't lie next to another
like these matches do.
Celibacy is a blanket
wrapped around myself
kind of keeping me warm
from a harsh storm
that use to be a lyrical breeze
caressing me.

MATCHES CONT'D.

In the restaurant
sitting across from you -
I would have liked to lie
along side - like these matches.

MEN, CALORIES AND THE IRS

Men, calories and the IRS -
three blisters to me.
Single, 40ish, female
living in the city,
having to carry my own grocery bags,
no one to share chores with
or to tell the small daily events,
no one to give me a shove
when I'm lazy.

Calories sneak in like the fog,
men - a parade of weird dogs,
and the IRS nipping at my heels.
Was my grandmother luckier
with her husband, lace and
hair in a bun?
She didn't worry about
her target pulse rate.
Just being proper
was all she had to do
to be successful.
Striving for independence
was a yoke
she didn't have to wear.

ON BEING VERY PRESENT
AND FOCUSED

Good talks -
like playing badminton
on a slightly warm
summer afternoon.
You'd hit wide the plastic birdie
Ping!
Then I'd return it
Ping!
And so,
back and forth,
looking to the air
Satisfaction when connecting
with our ideas
and thoughts.
I miss the back and forth
of our ideas and thoughts
on a slightly warm
summer afternoon
in the country.

OH, WE LIVE AS PIECES OF A PUZZLE

Oh, we live as pieces of a puzzle
fitted together tentatively
to be jumbled up anytime
by anyone.
We then lay scattered
separated and turned around.
We are disjointed
turned around and upside down.
Tomorrow maybe some hand
will settle us again.

Loving you is lying
Intoxicated
And oh so comfortable
In a velvet electric chair.

Making love with you
Flings me high
On a ferris wheel.

Lying next to you
I'm a tree
Covered with petals.

A beautiful woman
Just came to Meadowlark
But she's alone -
She is physically fit
Gorgeous
But still alone.

Hey, world!
You told me
If I was beautiful
And sexy
And wore high heels
With support stockings,
I wouldn't be alone.
Look at her -
She's all that
But still alone.

I remember my horse Kemptone
use to shy
and at first she threw me
to the ground.
But then after slow rides
I wouldn't fall off when she shied.
So with you
when you shy
I hope in time
I won't be thrown off
because we've had many long quiet rides.

You hang my faults
on the clothes line
one after another
displaying them
to the neighbors -
right in front of my window.

DOCTOR'S ORDERS

DOCTOR
11/8/1970

Doctor, I come to you
crumbs dried
stale
tasteless.
Can you somehow
glue together the pieces
with water as a potter does?
Please
don't cast me out
with a kick.

Your chair
holds me
and your 45 minutes
are a blanket
that wrap around me
and bring me comfort.

Doctor-
cut out the torment
the bleeding
the rotten.
Throw it away.
Cleanse me free
from the birds plucking sores.
You are so well.
Spread your health.

A thief in the night you were.
Tip toed into my chamber,
quietly.
Only flashlight of mammogram
spotted you.
Then!   I called upon
all exterminators.
Sirens, bright lights
to remove you
like an awful bat
in my living room.
Now you're gone.
Everything is back in place.
Do not return.

Cancer dog chasing me.
Surgery, lumpectomy removed threat.
But..WOW!..another snarling cancer dog
Returned
Suddenly
Scaring me
to run to Oncologist, mammogram
and surgeon.
Stop the barking dog cancer
that is threatening me.
Hurry!   Stop it -
Remove it.

MENOPAUSE

Snarling wolf thoughts
chasing like the wind
around corners
causing doors to slam
and mental windows to shake.
As the night deepens,
their fangs lengthen.
The bed
each little bump a mountain.
All night wolf thoughts
race along.
When day breaks,
they're found asleep
in a fuzzy, furry huddle.

Cancer you are a time monster
greedily eating up my plans
Ravishing -
Ravishing my freedom.
Tethering me to appointments
like a slave,
While you chomp on my hours.
But!
I escape and add more time
to end my life.
So I conquer you -
You ugly Time Monster.

No cancer!
My breasts opened wide -
Doves flew out.
White doves
with wings opened wide.
No Cancer
No Cancer
echoes through my valleys.

PART I

All too often, I've been stuck in traffic -
Cancer, radiation, long viruses.
Now an injury has shut down
Flow of my life.
My list of goals
gathering dust.
I hope I will live extra years
to make up for
being stuck in traffic.

PART II

How come others sail along
on moonlight bay
with no detours?
No flat tires?
How come?

I feel good seeing Grace
At the hospital.
We both stop and enjoy meeting.
It is the stopping
that is so special.

I feel good very early
in the morning
before the world is awake.
Before even the garbage trucks
come and make their presence known.

Alas! My life is stuck in traffic.
Leg injury constipates movement.
I try and design a life
with super highways of activity
so I can accomplish
from point A to B.
But! Sometimes illness or accident
makes me feel stuck in traffic.

My sciatic pain
pain
and I cohabiting
in a frame too small
for the two of us
two mismatched roommates.
What cruel hand
placed us together.
I wish I could
leave you.

Am trying to learn how to feel
it is a beautiful world
even when in horrible pain
or deluged by losses.
It is a beautiful world
when I count my blessings
and look around for beauty.
When in pain tend to retreat
into my shell
way down into the dark part.
But trying to learn to feel
it is a beautiful world
even when in horrible pain
or deluged by losses.

San Francisco is dying
right in front of my eyes
Streets torn up
like on a hospital operating table
Construction workers look like surgeons.
We stand around the bed of this
Old timers - old friends of San Francisco
The heart beat is slowing
The pulse of the true San Francisco fading
A cancer like plight is taking over
High rises, Uber, Lyft, and bikes
Eating at the calm once was here.

MEDICAL TO-DOS

8/27/2017

My life so full
of medical to do's
floss teeth
clean eye glasses
do physical therapy exercises
take meds and vitamins.
Medical to do's
termites eating
at the fabric of my time.
When is there time
to have plenty of time
to do as choose?
When is there time
plenty of time
to just do nothing?
To splash shining silver minutes
around me
in a refreshing way?

DOCTOR, PLEASE!

8/28/2018

Doctor, please do not tell me anything
else that would be good for me.
I'm terribly exhausted doing it all
and need to just rest
and not strain to do well.
Just need to absorb
and calibrate
and do nothing new.
Hope you can understand.
I am seriously on overload
and cannot take on anything new.

DOCTOR SQUARE DANCE

8/26/2019

Round and round
Allemande left and right
I spin to a doctor
He holds my hand
and passes me on
to the next doctor
who bows and
passes me on to another doctor
we hold hands
go in a circle
Then he passes me on
to the next doctor.
Doctor square dance.

BOTHERSOME BODY

10/31/2019

Wanting to climb to rocky terrains
and skip over all the rough terrains
but Instead, need to stand at the ridge
hanging-on tight to my young companion.
Wish could have
Complete body replacement
Except for my smile,
Heart and soul.
Wish could simply step out
of this jalopy body
like a caterpillar does
spread my wings and fly high.

VERY BUSY BEAVER ME

1/2/2020

Very full time body maintenance work
I'm feeling like the very busy beaver
at Brown Ledge Camp
whose whole existence
was plugging up holes
in the potentially declining lake.
If it wasn't for all his
plugging up leaks with logs,
the sinking lake would have disappeared.
So here I am busy going to doctors,
doing exercises trying to eat healthy
Flossing, flossing, flossing
To keep the lake of me
full and alive.
Busy beaver am I
Plugging only up the holes
of the sinking lake.

MENDING MY INSIDES

I'm mending my insides.
Fishermen's nets spread out
in the sun.
The breeze gently ruffles them.
They are not working now
just resting
and drying out.
The fishermen sew up
the broken parts
The healing sun warms --
And so my insides are resting
Meditation and white light
dry out the pain.
My Tagamet pills
stitching together the parts.

TIME FOR SPACE
& NATURE

REDWOODS, THERE WAS THAT TIME

11/1963

Slowly and patiently
From that in you which was still alive.
Til now you are gallant and admirable.
You give me strength and solace
As I make my pilgrimage to your feet
And bow with respect.
Yet, I see the burnt out area
That is still a part of you,
Know and understand
There was that time
That hungry fire ate at your insides
Leaving you hollow and empty.

I CALL TO THE REDWOODS

11/1963

I call to the redwoods,
"Sally Love Saunders loves you"
wanting their green branches
to soak up the message
while black stumps listen.
I love being among the redwoods
They tranquilize me!

AN IMAGE

8/17/1965

The day is drowsy
Slowly,
The sun lays its head down
On the horizon
And gently
The wind covers it
With night's black blanket
Bedecked with sequins.

CANADIAN GEESE

10/7/1994

Canadian Geese in military form
fly across the horizon.
Their straight black line
reminds me of a Navajo's
weaving shuttle going
from side to side
leaving a dark pattern
on the loom of the sky.

MOTHER MOON

1/5/2001

Mother moon
all night long
cradles me in her arms.
Softly sings lullabies
and Spirituals.
The trees listen.
The smooth blanket of the bay
Neatly folded aside.
The moon's arms
around me comforting.
Humming she soothes me
all night long.

INDIAN SUMMER IN SAN FRANCISCO

8/26/2005

September soon will visit
with too sunny days,
heat too high
and sweat drawn.
I prefer your sisters -
July and August
with cool days,
calm fog
and chance to cover up
with old jackets.
September I dread your visit.
Please tread lightly.
I'm older now
more frail.
No longer want to be in sun.
Your beaches here forbid me
from swimming.
Please don't stay long
and invite your sister's
Fog and Overcast to visit.

MISSING THE FOG

6/13/2006

Missing the fog
I call to it for return
like calling for a lost kitten.
"Here kitty, kitty, kitty"
Hoping it will return
under Golden Gate Bridge.
I think too much sun
and city noises
keep it from returning.
Perhaps tonight
when it is quiet,
the gray fog cat
will creep under the bridge
again
and sprawl down on the bay.
I certainly hope so.

DOLPHIN IN THE BAY

8/16/2008

Dolphin in the bay
day after day
I visit you -
You are there
dancing - spinning.
Only part of you is visible
Only bits of you but so beautiful.
And so with others -
I see and enjoy
only bits.
Others may see other parts
feel what is not for me
to feel.

Out of reach
but there daily
frolicking in the bay.
It is I who due to laziness
misses a day or so
of our connection
connecting with just a piece
a fraction - a slice.

DOLPHIN IN THE BAY   CONT'D.

Oh hum -
Oh - shucks
or okay.
Dolphin
I just see part of
someone beautiful and shiny.

It is 1 a.m. or 2 a.m.
or 3 a.m. or 4 a.m. my
pilot light is burning.
Quiet even sirens are asleep.
Every cell in me is alive
and humming.
Ready to create - to write.
Something so very juicy
about very early morning
when I wake.

A CREEKY DOOR
7/24/2012

In afternoons usually around 2
the doors would slam shut
and then there would be quiet.
Here in S. F. in afternoons
usually around 2
my doors slam
from afternoon winds
and I'm taken back
to Cape Cod as a child
in summer time.

I see you there
round faced moon
peeking in my window
as I sleep.
Your face
so perky and round.
But you choose
to not send warmth
just look at me
with your very round face.
I'm cold and could use warmth.
A yellow blanket of your rays
Would feel so nice
But you choose to just stare
with your perfect face.

It's that time in early morning
when creepy monster thoughts
dance wearing black
and I am still and motionless -
but eyes wide and round.
The dance of creepy thoughts
while dissonant screeching music plays.
My only movement is shivering
even breathing stops.

SWEET MOON

11/23/2013

A poem is kicking loudly
in my womb
like drumming noise
wanting to be heard.
The kicking poem about
how when I'm injured
and in pain.
The moon comes more often
to look in on me.
Yes, the moon visits me more often
when I'm injured and in bed
Sweet moon.

I'm looking for my companion the moon
he is nowhere to be found
guess he is busy sweeping clouds
of dust away
to set stage for rain.
The moon my most frequent visitor
while sick and lying in bed.
He comes unannounced and stares at me
as I sleep.
Sometimes he brings his grandchildren
the lively stars.

The moon is not here.
He has totally left.
Visitor I now have is foghorn
who is pompous
and too talkative
but I can't shut him up.
My moon friend
comes quietly and sits by me
hums and sends sweet vibes.
I miss my moon friend.

Just one little star
or is it a sheep
in the sky?
But mostly empty sky
empty of golden moon light
empty of smiling moon face.
Just one lonely lost star
lost from its galaxy family
all alone in cold metal sky.
He has totally left.

DANCERS IN THE PARK

6/11/2017

Trim pointed pointer dog
studied moves - so carefully
no extra skin -
Pointer dog pointing
at a tai chi artist
who also measures movements.
They seem to be so aware of each other
As though partners dancing in space!

MOON POEM

7/26/2018

PART I

Alive moon bouncing from
In front of us to
Behind the trees hides
Lively moon's arms out stretched
Wanting to hug.
We drive along
The moon plays peek-a-boo.
Come back moon
I miss you
Moon waited for us
when we went into the grocery store.
Now it is back
and looks like a giant pizza.
Moon bounces along by our side
Youthful energetic moon staring at us
hanging still and staring
The moon has turned into a wine picture
Pouring golden wine
making me light and giddy.

MOON POEM PART II

Old moon -
I'll still hang by you
you have lost body parts
and gotten old and wrinkled.
No more do you radiate energy
I am old too -
but you have always been my friend
and we will always be friends.

REDWOOD BARK

(San Mateo Skyline Blvd.)

12/29/2018

Redwood bark looks dark and velvety
in the shade.
Electric pompous trees.
Bright sun on tree trunks
making loud clangs of beauty.
Pompous grasses laughing
and giggling or chuckling
like hens in a hen house.
Silver on top of silver beach
with waves splashing more silver.

REDWOODS STAND TALL

1/24/2019

Redwoods stand tall
Branches holding hands.
Birds come and whisper
to me welcome.

VISITING THE OCEAN

2/22/2019

Visiting-by with Ocean
Listening - laughing
enjoying the company
of the Oceans waves
and foam.
The Ocean seems to me
to be enjoying visiting laughing
enjoying being with me.
We are best friends
We don't have to do anything
Just enjoying each other's company

SHARING AIR WITH REDWOODS

(Written at the Botanical Garden, S.F.)

9/4/2020

Sharing air with redwoods
the ferns reflect my lungs
breathing in and out
while a crow visits us.
A meditation grove
in the redwoods,
calming and centering.
No news flashes
no emails
knocking at my door.
Here in this timeless place.
Thank you, world
for respecting my privacy.
Fresh air washing off
pollen's dust.
I'm living in that zone
strived for in meditation classes.

Green patches of leaves
transfusion of calm
There is a currency
I'd like to join into.
The plug that goes into
the outlet You
and electricity,

SHARING AIR WITH
REDWOODS CONT'D.

though invisible,
can live.
I like it when we connect
and there is light
and connection.
I like it when we connect
and electricity can happen.
In the redwoods
it feels like
I'm lying on my back
in flat, cool water.
Arms outstretched
Body bobbing
on a mattress of gentle waves.

5 A.M.

The wind is asleep.
The moon has dark blanket
pulled up around its ears.
Only bright blond hairs leaks
out the side.
Winds inside my mind
are at rest too.
No dust flying across
the surface of my brain.

FOGHORN

9/18/2020

Fog is galloping in
I'm taking a cool fog bath.
Fog singing to me
I sing to the fog.
(I also talk to crows and
moo to cows.)
Foghorns crying
and gets an answer
But calls for more.
Woman fog horns begging
If I change my tone,
will you come to me?
Woman fog horns beg
I want to fall
into your foghorn arms
Singing fog horns
treble key in harmony
and bass key
all in harmony.
They harmonize to me
softer than before.
Foghorn now
is a cow
or a yodeler
from the Alps.

FOGHORN   CONT'D

I'm soaking in the symphony
of foghorns
and sitting in prayer position.
While chanting with
foghorns chanting.

THE FOG AND ME

10/9/2020

Silver lacy fog
drapes over
the shoulders of the hills.
Fog absorbing stress.
I want to dive
into the arms of the fog
and roll with it.
Also, I want to take
the silk quilt of the fog
and wrap it all around me.
Fog makes me so happy
to be around it
and in it and with it.
Exciting to be with fog
and have it pat my cheek.
Together we become one,
the fog and me.

DOCKSIDE

My boat is in a harbor these days.
It's rocking gently
and not traveling any place.
It feels good just to be
in a harbor
with the charts folded
and the compass ignored.
There aren't any train whistles
haunting me in the night.
I'm not concerning myself
about the morning
when distant winds will call me
and far away sands will beckon.
Questions of future plans -
buzzing flies I brush away.
I'm not looking around the bend.
There are no winds pushing me to move.
It's enough for now
to be very much settled
here in this harbor
with my sails folded
and my engine off.
Soft waves lapping
against my sides so very soothing.
My boat is in a harbor these days
and not traveling any place.

I LOVE MY DOG

I love my dog
because she doesn't
have to do anything.
She just is.
She doesn't take on
a lot of projects.
She refuses to contaminate
herself in the polluted stream
of nonsense.
She is simply herself.
Her joys greeting me and
going for walks.
She doesn't concern herself
about tomorrow.
She is
and that is enough.

A BIG BRASS PLATE

The full moon is a big brass plate
That hangs on the wall of the sky
For decoration.

HOW DIFFERENT

A sea gull that soars in beauty
Screams as if suffering great pain.
A buzzard that feasts on death
Is quiet and contented.

I wish I was a spider
able to spin a web
out of my being -
my inner being.
I'd step back
and watch my insides
glisten
in the sunlight!
A Navajo weaving a rug,
an artist making a mosaic,
balanced pattern.
How I wish I could make
a balanced art piece
out of my insides.

THE MOON

The moon
Weaves a spider's web
From grass to grass.
The moon
Lavishes velvet
Over the valley.
The moon on the ocean rolls
Like oil on water.
One can say a word
And it is gone.
But a word on mist
Can cling and haunt the area
Like the moon.

AGING GRATEFULLY

1/16/1990

Yesterday, I turned fifty.
There was a big party
and people said I looked younger.
When I turned 15,
people said I looked grown up.
It's nice to have friends
to help us through life's passages.

10/16/1994

As a child, I blew bubbles
with Bazooka Bubble Gum!
Big pink bubbles.
As an adult,
I have big plans,
very big plans.
Forever chewing the cud of ideas;
like a cow in the shade
on a hot summer afternoon.

AGING

7/26/2005

The mirror use to be kind.
Now it is like the mirror
at the old amusement park
that twists and distorts
me into grotesque forms.
Yikes!
The senior discounts;
Kleenex to wipe away sweat
from hot flashes.

Missing childhood days
no school - no appointments
Free day
Would go to neighbor's house
and ask if Janice could play.
Then we decided what we'd do
right then. -
Ideas so fresh -
like freshly baked bread.
Now I'm a senior citizen
having a lot of medical appointments.
I have to book ahead
then obey calendar.
Wish I could just go
and climb through
huge round cement tunnel under the road
and make noises that echoed.
I can feel dampness of the cement round tunnel.
Had to bend over then
to travel to the other side.
Now I'd probably have to slither through
while holding my breath.

Yesterday, or was it before yesterday
I was reading a book
In the shade of the barn
The writing glowed.
I felt sweet emotion.

1/22/2011

Now I am 71
Feel like can play
keys of my life
up and down piano keyboard.
Sometimes a crying toddler
Sometimes a teenager
interested in lipstick.
Sometimes my fingers move slowly.

SELF PORTRAIT

7/14/2012

So tiny so very tiny
sometimes invisible
but quaking and shivering
and blowing bubbles
from bazooka bubble gum.
My eyes have shrunk
from childhood
once blue now pond color.
Mostly invisible
mostly invisible.

BRIDGING THE GENERATION GAP

(Written for Sunday Evening Group)

9/12/2016

I know I can't dazzle you
with current love drama
and my gray hair and wrinkles
are no fun to look at
But underneath I'm just like you
swimming in the same river of
Compulsive Overeating Current.
Only you have managed to reach shore
and dry off
while I'm struggling to stay afloat.
Please, Please lend me a hand
and a towel.
I, on the other hand
have towels for you
when you need.

DOWNSIZING

3/17/2013

A poem or a song
should be written about downsizing.
When I was a teenager, the buzz-
word was junior prom.
Then it was talk about getting married
then having babies.
Now I'm in my 70's
and have many friends there too.
What do we talk about now?
DOWNSIZING!
Downsizing has created
a new look for my apartment.
Parts of it look new
like a minimalist would have.
Giving away treasures
to younger family or friends
insures they have a longer life.
Like at Easter time
now with my hunting
for places to put treasures.
Downsizing has its own beat
First music of act is slow
then it gets going and picks up speed.
Downsizing a song or a poem
should be written about DOWNSIZING.

BUCKETS

10/9/2013

When I was six
I had a tin bucket
that was colorful
and rusty.
It held sand
but not water.
Yet bucket and I
went to beach daily
to enjoy sun, water and sand.
Now I am old
I have a make believe bucket
a bucket list
of all want to do before die
before I kick the bucket
as when I was six
and had a bucket
This bucket has holes
so sometimes what I put in it
leaks out.
I can not control
what stays and what leaks out
because often sand leaks out with water.
So there has never been a bucket
in my life that holds
all I want to hold.

My mother used to say
you will die young
if you do not get more sleep
you will die young
if you don't eat all your vegetables
Well... I did not always
get proper amount of sleep
and still don't always eat
all my vegetables
But! I'm here to say
I did not die young!

JUST SMILES
7/18/2015

75. I am on the home stretch
Now what to do
with undone plans
and dreams?
Do I fold them neatly up
and put into a box
for next life?
or shrink and do in miniature?
Do I make a pretend-like
doll house of to-do plans?
To be on Broadway shrunk
into 15 minutes at a local cafe?
.75 I am on the home stretch
traveling fast.
What do I do with undone dreams?

CAN'T KEEP UP WITH MYSELF

11/5/2015

Can't keep up with myself
I say will give a lecture.
Then when the time comes,
I'm not up to it.
I invite someone over
and when the evening comes,
I don't want to do it.
But want to do something totally different.
I can't keep up with myself.
A taller self goes ahead.
The real younger self cannot catch up.

MUMMY

9/6/2017

Mummy, I am you
when you were me now.
Then I was young
and you were old.
Now I am old
like you used to be.
I am you
like you were
when
you were me now.

PHEW - NOW I'M 80!

11/15/2019

Phew - I am 80!
No longer
Have to worry if pregnant
and no longer
have to starve myself
to attract imaginary Mr. Right.
No longer
have to curl my eye lashes
or get legs waxed.
I'm eighty and can request
Telephone operators
To please talk slower.
I am eighty
Eight is my lucky number
and It will be with me for ten years

AGING ALL ABOUT LOSS

12/18/2019

Aging - all about loss
Like the fall off
of artichoke leaves
Green leaves that support us
drop off,
Then what created our beauty
drops off
until the heart
of the artichoke -
The best part.

TECH TODDLER

9/10/2020

So wanting to walk
the walk of technology
reaching for it-smiling
but then BOOM!
I tumble flat
on my face.
Tech Daddy Greg again
helps me up
and steadies me
and I try again
laughing
only to fall-
I cry
stomp my feet
But! merrily try again
to do the tech walk.
Someday
I will be grown up
tech walker,
But for now I am a tech toddler.

GROWING UP ON A FARM

10/28/2020

As a child growing up on a farm
Enjoyed so much going to hen house
with an empty basket
to collect eggs.
The pleasure of picking warm eggs
and holding them in my hand
enjoying the warmth
and placing in a basket.
Now I do not live on a farm
do not even in the country.
Just city living surrounded with concrete.
My egg gathering is writing poetry
like a settled feathery hen
I lay my poetry eggs
and then enjoy putting them
into my poetry basket:
modern day drop box is my
my basket for fresh warm poems.

AS A RAMBUNCTIOUS KID
11/14/2020

As a rambunctious kid
I was always told
to pipe down
Run around the house
because too energetic
to be at dinner table.
Now I'm a grown up child
And still rambunctious
Do I need to run
around the house
for 10 minutes?

LOVE BEING AN AUNT

11/28/2020

Love being an aunt
many times
to a tribe of nieces and nephews
and to great-nieces and nephews
Being an aunt-
I've enjoyed my nieces and nephews
from the start
and like reading a good book
watched them emerge and flower.
Love following their adventures
and life stages
You know,
some started off as serious adults
and now that they are older,
have become child-like
I'm enjoying their child spirit
What next?
what will unfold?
Like a colorful Advent calendar
they are
More windows will open.

PLANNING

Stitch   Stitch   Stitch
So many stitches to hold
my life together.
Basting
Pinning - re-setting
fittings.
Daydreaming; turning slowly
around in front of mirror.
I think of sewing machines
that can stitch so fast.
And I think of embroidery
with patient, calm women
where time is not the issue.

My life -
Combining colors
Seams
So it will fit
So it will be smooth.
I remember as a child
making doll clothes.
The pleasure was in the making
not in looking at the finished product.

Yarn unraveling
stitch after stitch
un-weaving - erasing patterns
until
it
stops.
My life unraveling
faster and faster.

TESTIMONIALS

I remember so well senior year, standing in the dark hallway outside my room talking to Sally, and her telling me that her intent in life was to be a poet. I was in awe, and never doubted her intent for a moment because even at such an early age, that's who Sally was - a poet. For her to know - and to already be - her future boggled my superficial mind.

I am in awe of Sally.

Love,
Lucy

Sally,

I celebrate your wonderful creativity and your excellent promotion of poetry in the SF area and beyond. What a wonderful legacy you have! We all appreciate you so much! Thank you for all you have contributed to CIF (Cultural Integration Fellowship) and the city's wonderful poetry events over the years. … Please say hi to your beloved poets for me.

And I send you a big "virtual hug" from WI. You are a light in the universe, carry on! All the best to you in your new year - may it be your best ever! Stay happy and healthy!

With much love and gratitude for your friendship!

As always,
Sandy

Sally Mallard

i'm coasting on a poetry pond
just one of many ducklings
who found a happy home
under the spread of your loving wings
though i've stayed a little longer than most
because i'm still tied to apron strings
and connected to the kind of spirit
that highlights the beauty in ordinary things

you nurture poems and people
protecting the eggs of our egos
from inside their fragile shells
while allowing them to crack open
to reveal their real potential
with words written, read and spoken

you've watched us hatch from year to year
lifted spirits and smoothed
the ruffles of our fears
so that we can confidently steer
our feelings and thoughts
through the murky and dark
until we reach waters clear
where ducklings ride the rhythmic waves
with Sally mallard floating on poetry bay

by Greg Pond

GRATITUDE

Greg - my poetry son. For countless years he attended my poetry workshops and readings. He very kindly went through all my 8,000 poems and selected ones for this book!

Leslie - for countless years has typed up my poems and organized them.

Rob - Has great regard for my work - always encouraging and path-finding for my work.

And to all the hospitals, government grants, students, friends, family, poets and publishers who have enjoyed and wanted my work throughout the years.